Sam the Sloth
FEELS SAD

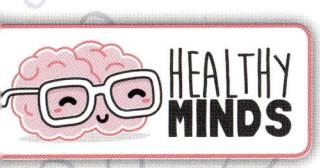

Written by **John Wood**

Illustrated by **Danielle Jones**

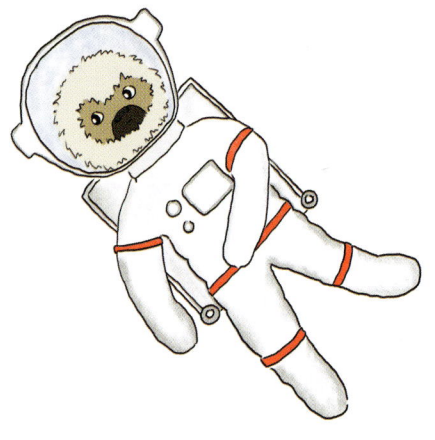

©2019
Book Life
King's Lynn, Norfolk PE30 4LS

ISBN: 978-1-78637-367-0

All rights reserved
Printed in Malaysia

A catalogue record for this book is available from the British Library.

Written by:
John Wood

Edited by:
Holly Duhig

Designed & Illustrated by:
Danielle Jones

With grateful thanks to Place2Be for their endorsement of this series.
These titles have been developed to support teachers and school counsellors in exploring pupils' mental health, and have been reviewed and approved by the clinical team at Place2Be, the leading national children's mental health charity.

THINGS TO THINK ABOUT...

Here are some questions to think about while reading this book:

What do you do when someone you know feels sad?

How can you tell if someone is sad? How does Sam look and behave when she's feeling sad?

Have you ever been sad before? Think about how Sam feels. Have you ever felt the same?

It's playtime. The children are outside with a kite. But Sam the Sloth is sitting on her own.

She doesn't feel like playing.

The kite is flying high above.

"Mind that tree, Gareth!"

shouts Matilda, but it's too late.

The kite is caught in the branches of the tallest tree.

"Sam, you are the BEST at climbing trees," says Matilda.

"Could you get the kite back?"

But Sam feels **sad**. Her hands and feet feel heavy.
She doesn't feel like climbing – she wants to go home.
She wants to make herself very small and very still.

"Let's stand on each other's shoulders," says Maya, at the bottom.

"I don't like this idea," says Gareth, at the top.

"There's no time to get the kite," says Matilda. "We need to cheer Sam up."

The children scratch their heads and think about what to do.

"Sometimes when I feel sad, I like to play my favourite game. Let's play space explorers!"

says Maya.

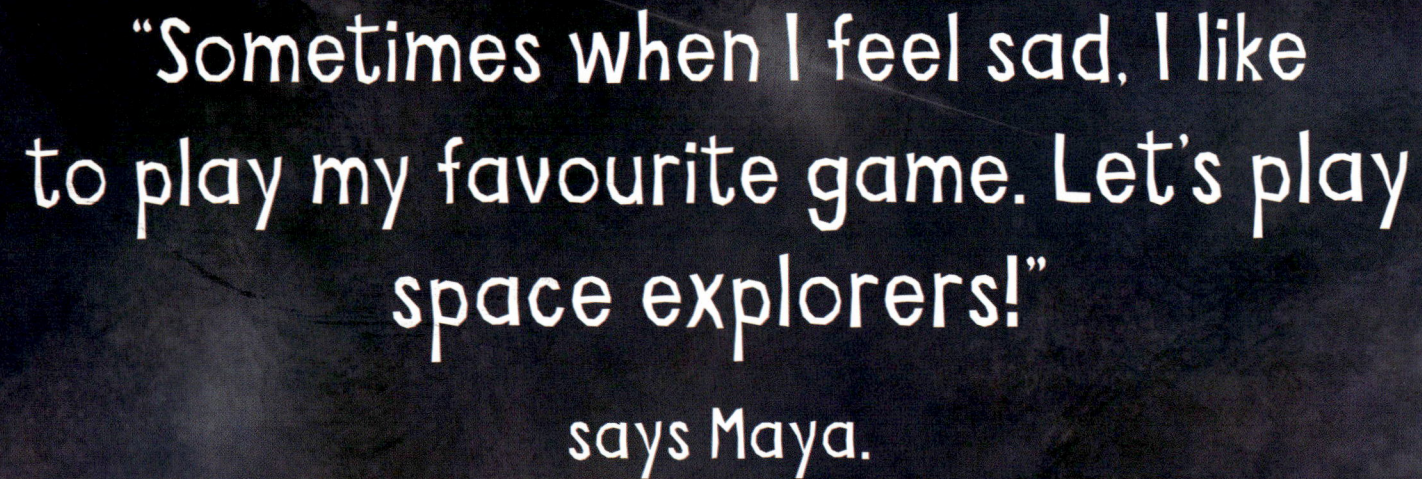

All of a sudden, there is a rustling above them.

The kite falls down and bounces off Matilda's head!

The children cheer.
Matilda throws the kite.

It soars high above...

...and lands in the second tallest tree!

"Not again!" says Wei. "Where's Sam?"

But Sam - who feels much better - has already climbed the tree!

She holds the kite and smiles as the children cheer again.

THINGS TO THINK ABOUT...

After reading this book, try answering these questions.

Can you think of any reasons why we might get sad? Why did Sam feel sad?

When you feel sad, do you like to be around friends, or be alone? Whatever you feel is OK.

How do you cheer yourself up when you feel sad? Who do you talk to when you feel sad?

"I miss my parents," says Sam.
"It's making me sad."

Everyone listens carefully.
Maya tells Sam that she misses her parents too sometimes. Sam is glad she is not the only one who feels sad from time to time.

Ms Bagley sees the mess and rushes over.
She sees Sam looking sad and still.

The children tell her that they have tried everything to make Sam feel better.

"These are all good ideas,"
says Ms Bagley.

"But sometimes it is best to talk about why we feel sad."

"Thanks," says Sam. "But I don't feel like painting right now."

Gareth runs around the corner.

"I've got the pai-"

Suddenly, Gareth tumbles over.
Poor Gareth has spilled paint over himself,
head to toe, and there is nothing
left to paint with.

"I know what to do,"
says Gareth, as he runs back inside.
"Sometimes when I'm sad, I like to paint."

The children go inside to grab paper
and bristly brushes. They race back outside
where Sam is still looking very small and sad.

"Sometimes when I feel sad, I just need to play some football,"

says Sam's friend, Wei.